On Your
Plate

Bread

Honor Head

W
FRANKLIN WATTS
LONDON•SYDNEY

First published in 2007 by Franklin Watts

Franklin Watts
338 Euston Road, London NW1 3BH

Franklin Watts Australia
Level 17/207 Kent Street, Sydney, NSW 2000

Copyright © Franklin Watts 2007

Created by Taglines
Design: Sumit Charles; Harleen Mehta, Q2A Media
Picture research: Pritika Ghura, Q2A Media

ISBN: 978 0 7496 76315

Dewey classification: 641.8'15

A CIP catalogue for this book is available from the British Library.

Picture credits
t=top b=bottom c=centre l=left r=right m=middle

Cover Images: Shutterstock, istockphoto and dreamstime.
Olga Shelego/ Shutterstock: 4, Juriah Mosin/ Shutterstock: 5, Felinda | Dreamstime.com: 6, Condor 36/ Shutterstock: 7,
Kenneth Chelette/ Shutterstock: 8, Joe Gough/ Shutterstock: 9, Graça Victoria/ Istockphoto: 10, rebvt/ Shutterstock: 11,
William Berry/ Shutterstock: 12mr, Mike Grindley/ Shutterstock: 12bl, hugo chang/ Istockphoto: 12br,
ANNAMARIA SZILAGYI/ Shutterstock: 13, Kharidehal Abhirama Ashwin/ Shutterstock: 14, Q2A Media: 15, Disorderly |
Dreamstime.com: 16, Aragorn | Dreamstime.com: 17, Pierre Janssen/ Istockphoto: 18, luminouslens/ Shutterstock: 19, Dumitrescu
Ciprian-Florin/ Shutterstock: 20, Elena Elisseeva/ Shutterstock: 21.

Printed in China

Franklin Watts is a division of Hachette Children's Books,
an Hachette Livre UK company.

Contents

What is bread?

Bread is made from flour. Grains of wheat are ground to make flour.

Golden wheat grows in huge fields.

The flour is mixed with water to make dough. Then yeast is added to make the dough rise.

dough

flour

 The dough is rolled into a ball and baked in the oven.

5

White bread

White bread is made with flour that uses only a small part of the wheat grain.

crust

 The outside of bread is called the crust.

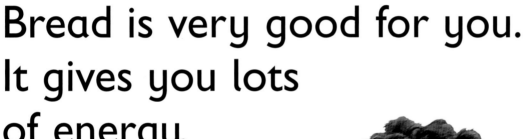

Bread is very good for you.
It gives you lots
of energy.

You should eat
some bread
every day.

7

Brown bread

Brown bread is made with flour that uses a part of the wheat grain called bran.

 Brown bread can taste nutty.

Try beans on toast for breakfast.

Bread can be toasted to make it crispy and crunchy.

Pitta bread

Pitta is a flat bread. It can be cut open to make a pitta pocket.

A pitta pocket can be stuffed with tuna and salad.

A pitta can be toasted and then sliced to make pitta fingers or wedges.

 Crispy pitta wedges with a dip are good to share with friends.

11

Bread rolls

A roll is like a small loaf of bread. Rolls can be cut in half and filled with salad, meat or cheese.

A roll is easy to eat and perfect for a lunchbox.

crusty roll

bagel

brown roll

Hamburgers and hotdogs are eaten with rolls.

 A roll stuffed with a hamburger and salad is a tasty meal.

Indian bread

In India, flat bread is used to scoop up food instead of a fork or spoon.

bowls of curry

puri

 Some Indian meals are served with bowls of curry and bread called puri.

Peshwari naans are filled with sweet foods such as coconut and sultanas.

Naans are flat breads. They can be stuffed with meat and vegetables.

Croissants

Croissants come from France. They are soft and flaky.

 Croissants are shaped like a crescent Moon.

Many people eat a croissant for breakfast with butter and jam.

 Croissants can be also be eaten with cheese and ham like a sandwich.

French stick

A French stick is a long, thin loaf of bread.

A French stick has a thick, crispy crust.

A chunk of French stick is good to eat with soup.

Sometimes people break off a bit of the bread to eat with their meal.

19

Pizza

The bottom of a pizza is made with the same dough that is used to make bread.

 Lots of tasty toppings can be added to a pizza.

A pizza is cooked in an oven. It can be eaten as a main meal with salad.

A slice of pizza is quick and easy to eat.

Things to do

Bread basket

Can you remember what these breads are called? Which ones are a French stick, brown bread and crusty rolls?

Match maker!

Can you match the two halves to find a pizza, a bagel and a croissant?

Make a meal!

Choose the bread to go with the meal below.

a) Try me with a bowl of warming soup.
b) Stuffed with tuna and salad I am great in a lunchbox.
c) Eat me with a spicy curry.

23

Glossary

bran
Bran is the part of the wheat grain that is good for you.

grains
At the top of the wheat stalk are seeds called grains.

ground
When grains are crushed and made into flour.

rise
Dough has yeast added and is then left to rise. The yeast makes the dough grow to about twice its size.

Index